Sonoran Desert Research Journal

Robin Johnson

CRABTREE
Publishing Company
www.crabtreebooks.com

D1445477

Crabtree Publishing Company
www.crabtreebooks.com

Author: Robin Johnson

Editors: Sonya Newland, Kathy Middleton

Design: Clare Nicholas

Cover design: Margaret Amy Salter

Proofreader: Angela Kaelberer

Production coordinator and prepress technician: Margaret Amy Salter

Print coordinator: Margaret Amy Salter

Consultant:

Written and produced for Crabtree Publishing Company by White-Thomson Publishing

Front Cover:

Title Page:

Photo Credits:

Cover: All images from Shutterstock

Interior: Alamy: p. 8t Tom Bean, pp. 14–15 Stone Nature Photography, p. 16b Robert Shantz, pp. 20–21 Rick & Nora Bowers, p. 21b Nature Collection, p. 29t Norma Jean Gargasz; Ron Dixon: p. 5r; Getty Images: p. 8b Annie Griffiths Belt; iStock: p. 19 ivstiv; Shutterstock: pp. 4–5 Jon Manjeot, p. 5l Kris Wiktor, p. 6 Tim Roberts Photography, p. 7t Martin Froyda, p. 7m Tom Tietz, p. 7b Anton Foltin, p. 9m Matt Jeppson, p. 9r Kevin_Hsieh, p. 10t Joseph Sohm, p. 10b CrackerClips Stock Media, p. 11t tntphototravis, p.11b Zack Frank, p. 12t Gabriel Walter Farmer 1, p. 12b Morphart Creation, p. 13t Jean-Edouard Rozey, p.13b Joshua Haviv, p.13l Wollertz, p. 14 photomaster, p. 15tl ira, p.15tr Captiva55, p.15b Benjamin B, p. 16 b Coalition for Sonoran Desert Protection, p. 16t Sherry Yates Young, p. 17t Jerry Horbert, p. 17bl Peter Milota Jr, p. 17br David Thyberg, p. 18t Tim Zurowski, p. 18b Tom Grundy, pp. 18–19 Gary L. Brewer, p.21t Natalia Kuzmina, p. 22t akramer, p. 22b oksana.perkins, p. 23t oksana.perkins, p. 24 ira, pp. 24–25 Michael Rosebrock, p. 25 lynea, p. 26 logoboom, p. 27 Tim Roberts Photography, p. 28 tishomir., p. 29b Anton Foltin; Wikimedia: p. 20 Bcexp, p. 23b U.S. Fish & Wildlife Service.

Library and Archives Canada Cataloguing in Publication

CIP available at the Library and Archives Canada

Library of Congress Cataloging-in-Publication Data

Names: Johnson, Robin (Robin R.), author.
Title: Sonoran Desert research journal / Robin Johnson.
Description: New York, New York : Crabtree Publishing Company, 2018. |
Series: Ecosystems research journal | Includes index.
Identifiers: LCCN 2017029505 (print) | LCCN 2017030427 (ebook) |
   ISBN 9781427119322 (Electronic HTML) |
   ISBN 9780778734918 (reinforced library binding : alkaline paper) |
   ISBN 9780778734970 (paperback : alkaline paper)
Subjects: LCSH: Sonoran Desert--Environmental conditions-
   -Research--Juvenile literature. | Biotic communities--
   Research--Sonoran Desert--Juvenile literature. | Ecology-
   -Research--Sonoran Desert--Juvenile literature. | Sonoran
   Desert--Description and travel--Juvenile literature.
Classification: LCC GE160.S58 (ebook) |
   LCC GE160.S58 J65 2018 (print) | DDC 577.0972/17--dc23
LC record available at https://lccn.loc.gov/2017029505

Crabtree Publishing Company

www.crabtreebooks.com   1-800-387-7650

Printed in Canada/082017/EF20170629

Published in Canada
Crabtree Publishing
616 Welland Ave.
St. Catharines, Ontario
L2M 5V6

Published in the United States
Crabtree Publishing
PMB 59051
350 Fifth Avenue, 59th Floor
New York, New York 10118

Published in the United Kingdom
Crabtree Publishing
Maritime House
Basin Road North, Hove
BN41 1WR

Published in Australia
Crabtree Publishing
3 Charles Street
Coburg North
VIC, 3058

Contents

Mission to the Sonoran Desert

Time to pack my sun hat and binoculars! I just found out I am going to the Sonoran Desert for my next research trip. A **desert** is an area of land that is very dry. It gets less than 10 inches (250 millimeters) of rain or snow each year. The Humans for Habitats group is sending me and other **wildlife biologists** to this desert in North America. My mission is to study how habitat loss is affecting the land, plants, and animals. I will look for signs of pollution, species that do not belong there, and other threats. I also hope to meet with people who are working to save the Sonoran.

The Sonoran Desert covers large parts of the southwestern United States and northwestern Mexico. It is about 100,000 square miles (260,000 square kilometers) in size.

I studied desert **biomes** so I could plan my trip. Deserts can be hot or cold. The Sonoran Desert is very hot! Summer temperatures can soar to 118 degrees Fahrenheit (48 degrees Celsius). Most deserts have only one short season in which heavy rains fall. The Sonoran Desert is different because it has two rainy seasons. There are thunderstorms and heavy rains in the hot summer months. Lighter rains fall in the cool winter months. Higher rainfall means that the Sonoran has more types of plants and animals than any desert in North America. I was hoping to see them all.

I will be hot on the trail of lizards called Gila monsters and other animals in the Sonoran Desert.

CALIFORNIA   ARIZONA

Colorado River

Algodones Dunes

Mexicali

Phoenix

Gila River

Yuma
Yuma Desert

Colorado
Desert

Santa Catalina
Mountains

USA

Tucson

USA-Mexico border

MEXICO

Guaymas

Santa Rosalia

Pacific Ocean

☐ Sonoran Desert

Field Journal: Day 1

Phoenix, Arizona

My research team met in Phoenix, Arizona. Phoenix marks the northern edge of the Sonoran Desert and is the largest city in this **ecosystem**. We set up camp and changed into cool, light-colored clothing. Then we loaded up drinking water and set out in trucks to explore the area. I was glad I had decided to come here in spring. Plants will be in bloom now and animals will be on the move. Some desert animals are not active during the winter, and many animals stay inside their homes in summer to beat the heat. Even now, some animals will be hiding from the hot desert sun. It will take patience—and a little luck—to spot them.

I looked out the airplane window as we got close to Phoenix. I was surprised to see how far the city spread into the desert.

The first thing I noticed was how huge the city was. It spread into the desert for miles. Many plants and animals are losing their natural habitats as Phoenix continues to grow. I was pleased to visit a large preserve in the city, however. A preserve is an area of land where wildlife is protected. I was lucky enough to spot a coyote and a chuckwalla there. These animals have colors and markings that help them blend in with their desert surroundings. That makes it harder for **predators** to find them.

Coyote.

Chuckwalla.

Phoenix is a huge, sprawling city. It stretches about 518 square miles (1,340 square kilometers) into the Sonoran Desert. It is the sixth-largest city in America—and growing fast.

We will travel by truck and stay on the roads and trails. Going off the road could harm plants, animals, and their natural habitats.

7

Field Journal: Day 2

Hassayampa River Preserve

Today we drove an hour outside the city to the Hassayampa River Preserve. A stream flows through the preserve all year round and creates an oasis. An oasis is a place in a desert with water and lush, green plants. Desert fan palms and all sorts of bushes and flowering plants grow near the river here. I walked through cool forests of towering cottonwood and willow trees. This is one of the most threatened types of forest in North America. I'm so glad that these rare trees are protected here in the preserve.

---

natstat STATUS REPORT ST456/part B

Name: Cottonwood-willow forests (*Populus fremontii* and *Salix gooddingii*)

Threats:
Habitat loss.

Numbers:
Not applicable.

Description:
Fremont cottonwood and Goodding willow trees only grow along rivers and streams in the Southwest. They provide food and habitats for birds, rodents, and many other animals. Their roots hold on to the soil, which helps keep riverbanks from **eroding**. Most of these important forests were lost when people changed the flow of rivers in the desert.

Status: Decreasing.

8 Attach photograph here ➡

I observed all kinds of animals as I walked along the river. Many of them make their homes here because water is hard to find in the desert. I spotted a Gilbert's skink resting on a rock. It darted under a log when it saw me. I also heard the scream of a zone-tailed hawk as it soared high above me. A willow flycatcher was perched on a branch nearby. I watched the little bird catch insects that flew past it. To my surprise, I even spotted a rare desert pupfish! These small, bony fish are found only in the Sonoran Desert. Sadly, they have lost most of their river habitats and are now endangered.

Gilbert's skink.

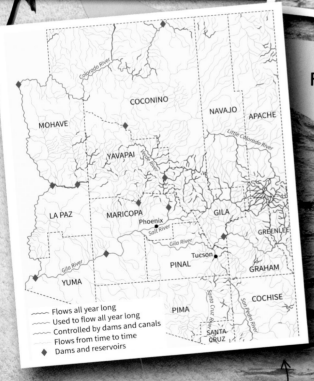

This map shows how rivers in one area of the Sonoran Desert have been changed by dams and canals.

People built dams and canals up the rivers to bring water to their cities and farms. This cut off the flow of water through the Sonoran Desert. About 90% of the riverbank habitats in the desert have been lost or damaged in the past 100 years.

9

Phoenix to Saguaro National Park

We packed up camp and headed south into the heart of the Sonoran Desert. We stopped at a **reservation** on our way. Native Americans have lived in the desert for thousands of years. The ancient Hohokam peoples built miles of canals on the Gila River. They used the canals to carry water through the desert. They grew cotton, beans, corn, and many other crops. I looked down at the dry, cracked soil at my feet. It was hard to imagine crops growing here. Now, dams built farther up the river have caused it to run dry in most places.

Many Native Americans live in cities and on reservations in the Sonoran Desert. This woman is a member of the Navajo Nation.

I saw some art carved on rocks by ancient Hohokam peoples. I will research what the symbols mean.

We set up camp near the city of Tucson. Then we headed to Saguaro National Park to study the huge cactuses that grow there. I examined some saguaro cactuses up close. It is easy to see how these plants have **adapted** to survive in the desert. They have thick, fleshy stems that hold a lot of water. The cactuses store this water for periods when it does not rain. The plants are covered in sharp spines which protect them from **herbivores**. I ran into a scientist from the Desert Research Learning Center. He pointed out some ironwood, palo verde, and mesquite trees. The trees were acting as nurse trees for young saguaros. Nurse trees are large, fast-growing trees that provide shelter for smaller, slow-growing plants.

← Cactus wrens, Gila woodpeckers, white-winged doves, and many other birds make their homes in saguaro cactuses.

natstat STATUS REPORT ST456/part B

Name: Saguaro cactus (Carnegiea gigantea)

Threats:
Habitat loss and collecting.

Description:
Saguaro cactuses are huge, tree-like plants found only in the Sonoran Desert. In the United States, saguaros are threatened by cities spreading into their habitats. This is called encroachment. In Mexico, saguaros are losing their habitats as space is made for cattle ranches, which need a lot of land for pasture.

Numbers:
Unknown, but decreasing.

Status:
Threatened in Mexico; least concern in the United States.

Attach photograph here ➡

Field Journal: Day 4

Santa Catalina Mountains

I got an early start today and biked all the way up Mount Lemmon. It is one of the sky islands here in the Sonoran Desert. A sky island is a single mountain that is surrounded by land that looks very different from it. Various plants and animals are found as you go higher up the mountain. The weather is cooler and wetter there. I passed through several biomes as I made my way slowly to the top. I stopped to write down some species I spotted along the way—and to catch my breath!

Sightings

I spied a big American black bear walking through the forest. These bears eat mainly berries and other plant foods. But I still pedaled my bike a little faster!

Cactuses and small shrubs dotted the base of the mountain. I had seen these plants before in the hot, dry desert biome. The landscape began to change slowly as I climbed the mountain. I cycled through swaying grasses. Then I passed through walnut, oak, and other **deciduous** trees. Arizona gray squirrels darted from branch to branch. I climbed higher and higher up the mountain until at last I reached the top. I identified pine, spruce, fir, and other **conifers** there. I looked up at the tall green trees and breathed in the cool mountain air. I could hardly believe I was still in the Sonoran Desert!

I saw an acorn woodpecker hiding nuts in a tree.

natstat STATUS REPORT ST456/part B

Name: Thick-billed parrot (Rhynchopsitta pachyrhyncha)

Description:
Large flocks of thick-billed parrots used to visit the mountains in southeast Arizona. They made their homes in the branches of pine trees and ate the pine seeds. Now these rare birds are found only in mountains in Mexico because of encroachment and **poaching**.

Threats:
Habitat loss and illegal pet trade.

Numbers:
2,000–2,800 mature birds.

Status:
Endangered.

Attach photograph here ➡

13

Field Journal: Day 5

Buenos Aires National Wildlife Refuge

Today I visited a wildlife refuge near the border of Mexico. I met a scientist who is breeding a rare bird species in **captivity** there. The masked bobwhite quail lost its habitat when people built large cattle ranches. The quails became extinct in the United States. Scientists at the refuge are raising the birds in captivity to release them into the wild again. I was excited to see this endangered species back in its natural habitat. I watched and waited quietly for hours. At last I spotted a quail hiding in the tall grass!

I was hoping to see a jaguar at the wildlife refuge but knew that it was unlikely. A jaguar is a rare species of large wild cat that is only seen from time to time in this part of the desert. I scanned the area with my binoculars. I could not see any spotted cats, but I did see a deer dashing through the grass. Was it running away from a jaguar, bobcat, coyote, or other predator? Although I did not see any jaguars, my luck did improve. I spotted a rare desert tortoise inching its way along the ground. These vulnerable animals are threatened by illegal hunting and off-road vehicles.

Desert tortoises spend most of their time in underground homes to escape the heat. They can live up to 80 years if people do not destroy their habitats.

natstat STATUS REPORT ST456/part B

Name: Jaguar (Panthera onca)

Threats:
Habitat loss and hunting.

Description:
Jaguars are apex predators. They are at the top of the food chain and have no natural enemies. Jaguars are important because they keep the numbers of the animals they hunt from becoming too large for the habitat to support.

Numbers:
80–120 in the Sonoran Desert, mostly in Mexico.

Status:
Endangered in the United States.

Attach photograph here ➡

Field Journal: Day 6

Tucson, Arizona to Guaymas, Mexico

Today we drove a long way down to the city of Guaymas in Mexico. The city sits on the southern edge of the Sonoran Desert. Along the way, I noticed wildlife bridges and tunnels built across the highway. These structures allow animals to cross over and under the road safely and avoid being hit by cars. We crossed the border into Mexico and drove through miles of dry, flat land. I spotted a greater roadrunner that was also on the move. This bird runs along the ground so fast, it is one of the few animals that can catch a rattlesnake! I was hoping to see a Mexican gray wolf too. But, like the jaguar, these endangered animals are hard to find these days.

This wildlife bridge has cactuses and other plants on top to make it look like the desert to animals.

There are fewer than 100 Mexican gray wolves left in the wild. People often kill these wolves to protect their farm animals.

I observed teddy bear cholla, mesquite, and other **native** plants as we made our way south. I also saw plenty of buffelgrass. This shrubby African grass is an **invasive species** in the Sonoran Desert. It was brought here about 50 years ago for cattle to eat. Buffelgrass is a problem because it spreads quickly and covers the ground like a thick carpet. It crowds out native plants, which must compete with the grass for water. Buffelgrass catches fire easily and enables flames to spread through the desert.

↑ The teddy bear cholla sounds cuddly, but it is not! This cactus is covered in sharp spines.

There are often thunderstorms during the summer rainy season. Lightning can strike buffelgrass and set it on fire. Most native plants have not adapted to survive the flames.

Sightings

I spotted a black-tailed jackrabbit resting in the shade of a bush. These hares are food for many desert **carnivores**.

Field Journal: Day 7

Nacapule Canyon, Mexico

Today I hiked through Nacapule Canyon. The canyon is a deep, narrow gap carved into the land. It was so cool and shady at the bottom of the canyon. It felt good to be out of the blazing sun for a while! Streams run all through the canyon and make pleasant oases in the desert. I bent down to fill my bottle with water. That's when I saw a canyon tree frog sitting beside the stream. I thought it was a rock until it started to hop away! And we weren't the only animals looking for a cool drink. I observed a Harris's antelope squirrel, a broad-billed hummingbird, and many other animals near the stream.

The Harris's antelope squirrel uses its tail to help shade its body from the desert sun.

Canyon tree frog.

I made my way slowly through the canyon. I climbed over rocks, explored dark caves, and squeezed through narrow openings. Then I stopped to rest by a pond under a leafy palm tree and listened to the sweet song of a canyon wren. There were all kinds of lush, green plants growing here. But it was a strangler fig that caught my eye. It was interesting to see how this tree has adapted to grow in a shady part of the desert. The strangler fig gets its name from the way it wraps its branches tightly around other trees.

Strangler fig seeds grow on the high branches of trees so they can get the sunlight they need. The roots of strangler figs wrap around the **host** trees and stretch down to the ground. The stranglers steal water and other resources from the hosts, and take their place over time.

Field Journal: Day 8

Guaymas, Mexico

I decided to rest up today and take an overnight ferry across the Gulf of California. The boat did not leave until late at night. That gave me a chance to see some **nocturnal** creatures in their natural habitats. Many desert animals rest during the day when the weather is hottest. They come out to look for food when the sun goes down and the temperature drops. I was excited to watch the desert come alive after dark!

Sightings

I saw a Merriam's kangaroo rat collecting plant seeds in its pouch. This little rodent gets all the water it needs from the seeds it eats.

I watched a great horned owl swoop down and catch a white-throated woodrat.

The moon was full tonight. It gave me just enough light to observe some busy nocturnal animals! I saw a rare lesser long-nosed bat drinking nectar from a saguaro cactus. Not far away, a herd of wild pig-like animals called peccaries was rooting in the ground for food. I even heard the sound of a western diamondback rattlesnake. It shook its tail to warn me to keep clear. It worked! I stayed far away from the big, **venomous** reptile.

Peccaries.

natstat STATUS REPORT ST456/part B

Name: Lesser long-nosed bat (Leptonycteris yerbabuenae)

Threats: Habitat loss.

Description:

Lesser long-nosed bats are important desert pollinators. Pollinators are animals, insects, and birds that spread pollen from one flower to another. The bats use their long snouts to reach deep into saguaro flowers and drink nectar. Pollen sticks to their hairy heads and gets spread across the desert when the bats fly to other cactuses.

Numbers: Unknown.

Status: Endangered.

Attach photograph here ➡

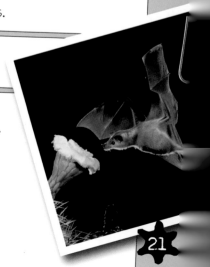

Field Journal: Day 9

Santa Rosalia to Mexicali, Mexico

Our boat docked early this morning. Then we were back on the road again. We headed up north along the Baja California Peninsula. The peninsula is like a long finger of land reaching out into the sea. We drove through protected areas called El Vizcaíno and the Valley of the Cirios. There are plants and animals there that are not found anywhere else in the world. I saw tall, spiny boojum trees and thick, twisted Baja elephant trees. I even spotted a rare peninsular pronghorn before it turned tail and ran away.

We stopped at a rare forest of Mexican giant cardons. I gazed up at the tallest cactuses in the world.

The peninsular pronghorn is one of the fastest land mammals in the world. I was lucky to spot one standing still!

Boojum trees.

We left the parks and drove north along the coast. I was thrilled to see hundreds of birds feeding and nesting on shore. There were herons, pelicans, sandpipers, and other birds as far as the eye could see. We passed through a number of towns that dotted the coast. I was disappointed to see people tossing trash on the ground and driving cars on the beaches. Visiting an ecosystem can help people learn how to protect it. But it can also harm the plants and animals that live there.

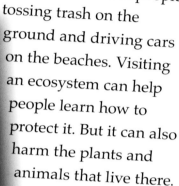

← Brown pelicans.

natstat STATUS REPORT ST456/part B

Name: Peninsular pronghorn (Antilocapra americana peninsularis)

Threats:
Habitat loss and hunting.

Description:
Peninsular pronghorns are deer-like animals. They are found only in this part of the Sonoran Desert. Most pronghorns lost their habitat when the land was turned into cattle ranches. Now scientists are breeding them in captivity to help boost their numbers.

Numbers:
About 200 in the wild.

Status:
Critically endangered.

Attach photograph here ➡

Field Journal: Day 10

Mexicali, Mexico to Algodones Dunes, California

This morning we crossed back into the United States and drove through the Yuma Desert. This is the hottest, driest part of the Sonoran Desert. It was such a change from the thriving landscape we saw yesterday! There was nothing to see but miles and miles of sand with creosote bushes here and there. Creosote bushes have adapted to very long periods without water. They have tiny, waxy leaves that help prevent water loss. I noticed some dead bushes along the way, however. Even these desert survivors are threatened by **climate change**.

Creosote bush. ↑

Off-road vehicles can harm plants and animals living in the Algodones Dunes.

The climate of the Sonoran Desert is becoming hotter and drier than ever before. There is less rain and even fewer sources of water in the desert. The climate is changing because the burning of **fossil fuels** is contributing to an increase in the temperature of land, air, and water around the world.

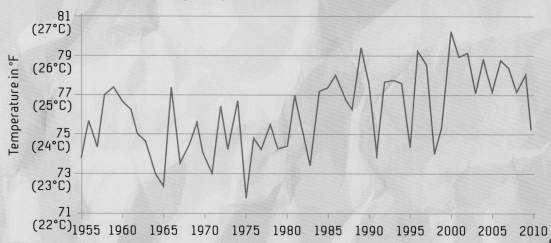

Average spring temperatures in the Sonoran Desert, 1955–2010

Temperature in °F

81 (27°C)	
79 (26°C)	
77 (25°C)	
75 (24°C)	
73 (23°C)	
71 (22°C)	

1955 1960 1965 1970 1975 1980 1985 1990 1995 2000 2005 2010

Later we crossed the Colorado River into California. Now we were in the Colorado Desert. It was another desert name but still part of the big Sonoran Desert. I stopped to explore the Algodones Dunes. This is the country's largest **sand dune** system. Lizards, tortoises, and many other animals live in the shifting sands of this habitat. I was lucky to spot a little Andrew's dune scarab beetle scurrying along the ground. I also noticed tire tracks in the sand—bad news for the beetles.

Sightings

I watched a turkey vulture swoop down to the ground to eat a dead animal. These big birds help keep the ecosystem healthy by cleaning up animal remains.

Field Journal: Day 11

Coachella Valley, California

We headed to the Coachella Valley on the last day of our research trip. I was surprised to see lush fields growing all around. I wondered if I was still in the desert! A local farmer told me that this area of the Sonoran has been highly **irrigated**. The Coachella Canal brings water from the Colorado River to farms in the region. The water enables people to grow grapes, oranges, mangoes, dates, peppers, and other crops.

The Coachella Canal is 123 miles (198 kilometers) long. It irrigates nearly 60,000 acres (24,000 hectares) of farmland in California.

This huge oasis was created in the desert so people could live here. But at what cost to the ecosystem? I met with a researcher at the Palm Desert Center to find out. She explained that the Colorado River used to go right through the Sonoran Desert. It started in the mountains in Colorado and flowed all the way down to the Gulf of California. It carried water to many smaller rivers in the desert. Now dams and canals bring the water to farms and cities instead. Less water means that fewer plants and animals can survive in the hot, dry ecosystem.

Coachella Canal.

Final Report

Report to: HUMANS FOR HABITATS

OBSERVATIONS

My findings show that habitat loss is leaving many desert species out in the cold. Cities are spreading into the Sonoran Desert at an alarming rate. This is crowding out the native plants and animals. People have changed the natural flow of water into the desert for their own use. Less water in an ecosystem that is already hot and dry could mean disaster for the desert. And climate change, invasive species, and other threats are only making it worse.

FUTURE CONCERNS

There are plans for a solar power plant in the Sonoran Desert. Solar power is energy that comes from the sun. It does not pollute the air and is a **renewable resource**. But the power plant will cover about 3,700 acres (1,500 hectares) of land in the middle of the desert. Will this help or harm the plants and animals living in the ecosystem?